A Citizen's Guide to

The World Community

Sean Connolly

www.heinemann.co.uk/library
visit our website to find out more information about **Heinemann Library** books.

To order:
☎ Phone 44 (0) 1865 888066

▤ Send a fax to 44 (0) 1865 314091

💻 Visit the Heinemann Bookshop at www.heinemann.co.uk/library to browse our catalogue and order online.

First published in Great Britain by Heinemann Library, Halley Court, Jordan Hill, Oxford OX2 8EJ,
a division of Reed Educational and Professional Publishing Ltd.

Heinemann is a registered trademark of Reed Educational & Professional Publishing Limited.

OXFORD MELBOURNE AUCKLAND JOHANNESBURG BLANTYRE GABORONE IBADAN PORTSMOUTH NH (USA) CHICAGO

Designed by M2 Graphic Design
Indexed by Indexing Specialists
Originated by Ambassador Litho Ltd.
Printed in Hong Kong/China

06 05 04 03 02
10 9 8 7 6 5 4 3 2 1

ISBN 0 431 14490 7

British Library Cataloguing in Publication Data
Connolly, Sean, 1956 -
A citizen's guide to the world community
1. International relations - Juvenile literature
I. title II. The world community
327

Acknowledgements
The Publishers would like to thank the following for permission to reproduce photographs:
AFP/Corbis/Eric Feferberg p34; AKG Photos p9; Bettman/Corbis p11; Bridgeman Art Library/Stapleton Collection p7; The Independent p40; PA News p15;
Popperfoto/AFP p21; Popperfoto/Reuters/Russell Boyce pp2, 26; Popperfoto/Reuters/Fiona Hanson p23; Popperfoto/Reuters/Kevin Lamarque p28; The Purcell
Team/Corbis p39; Reuters/Corbis/Romeo Ranoco p33; Reuters/Ray Stubblebine p19; Rex Features pp4, 12, 37; Rex Features/Sipa Press p16.

Cover photograph reproduced with permission of UN/DPI.

Every effort has been made to contact copyright holders of any material reproduced in this book.
Any omissions will be rectified in subsequent printings if notice is given to the Publisher.

CONTENTS

Any words appearing in the text in bold, **like this**, are explained in the Glossary.

PART 1

INTRODUCTION
The world community and you

We live in a **global village**. How often have you heard that phrase? And yet, like many phrases that have been so overused that they no longer seem to mean much, it does have some truth to it.

The world today, at the beginning of the new millennium, is vastly different from the way it appeared at the beginning of the last century, and totally unrecognizable when compared with the dawn of the last millennium.

What accounts for this change, and the rapid pace at which it takes place? Many people would put the answer down to science and technology, with improved health care, computer access, air travel and instant communications at the top of the list. All of these factors and more have contributed to the modern world, bringing distant places closer, both in terms of travel and in communications. The global village, then, is often seen as a world in which business meetings can take place involving webcam links connecting board members in London, New York and Tokyo. Or perhaps it simply refers to the fact that people in a village in Peru can watch a World Cup football final live via a satellite television link.

But the term global village means more than simple measurements of distance or time. The varied nations that comprise the world have become far more 'related' to each other. International organizations give the tiniest countries a voice, offering them a chance to make warnings about global warming, **deforestation** or human conflict. Larger countries, such as the United Kingdom, once dictated terms to the rest of the world because of their economic or military power. Now, as these larger countries come to terms with global problems of pollution, over-population or the depleted ozone layer of the atmosphere, they listen to these 'smaller' voices and learn from them.

British troops, such as the peacekeeping forces in the Bosnian conflict of the 1990s, have been at the forefront of efforts to maintain international stability.

Lessons from history

It is not always in the nature of countries to behave for the good of everyone. Political analysts tend to see a country's motives as being purely selfish. The United Kingdom is no exception here, and even today's government leaders must 'sell' anything in terms of how it will benefit the British public (the voters). So, when the government signed a **treaty** calling for a union of European countries, the public was told that this move would create 'a stronger Britain in a wider Europe'.

The public does not always believe what it is told, however. US President Woodrow Wilson failed to persuade the US Congress to enter the League of Nations (a forerunner of the United Nations) after the First World War. Britain was a member, along with most other major European powers, but the organization was unable to stop the rise of Hitler and the Second World War. When that second global conflict ended, the great powers agreed to drop their political differences and to aim for **consensus** and peacekeeping.

Most of the international organizations outlined in this book were born in the period immediately after the Second World War. It was a particularly important time for the United Kingdom because the British Empire began to break up. Participation in new organizations became more important than 'going it alone', and these new bodies actually allowed the United Kingdom to create new policies – on a global level.

Structure of this book

This book covers three main areas. First there is an outline of the historical development of global organizations in the twentieth century – the bloodiest period in human history. This is followed by detailed accounts of these same organizations, providing reasons for why they exist, how they operate and what Britain's role in each of them is. Then there is an examination of some of the ways in which the government and other national bodies maintain Britain's image on the world scene. The book concludes with a look at what might happen in the future, and some questions to consider about Britain's role in the international arena.

FIND OUT...

Nowadays, we have access to more information about people and countries around the world than ever before. The Internet gives us access to huge amounts of information. Global news organizations gather information from around the world and broadcast it into our homes. They also provide information on the World Wide Web. Why not visit the websites of two of the biggest of such organizations: the BBC (www.bbc.co.uk) and CNN (www.cnn.com).

HISTORY
Alliances and empires

Wars and conflicts have been part of human life for centuries. Border disputes, disagreements over natural resources or trading routes, or simply a quest for **aggrandisement** have driven nations to start wars, time and again. The way in which a modern country behaves towards other countries – which in effect forms its foreign policy – depends on how much it has learnt from the lessons of the past. No country can exist in isolation, particularly in the age of multinational corporations and the Internet, and it is the relationship between different countries that is vital in efforts to maintain peace.

Europe has seen conflict since the time of the ancient Greeks and Romans, and earlier than that. But even some of these earliest wars showed the way in which states could set aside differences in order to co-operate against a common threat. Modern political analysts describe this strategy as the 'balance of power'. This theory basically suggests that aggression on the part of a state or an **alliance** of states can be discouraged by another alliance of equal or greater strength being formed. If one state is more powerful than another state, peace may be preserved by an alliance of the weaker states.

Preserving the balance

One of the earliest examples of this balance of power strategy was the creation of the Peloponnesian League in ancient Greece. None of the League's members could restrain Athens alone, but together they aimed to persuade the Athenians against using aggression, or, if that failed, to defeat them in battle. This same formula was clearly spelled out in the sixteenth century by the Italian political thinker Francesco Guicciardini, who noted that the goal of Florence's policy was to prevent the domination of the Italian peninsula by any single city-state.

England adopted this strategy not long after Guicciardini was writing. European powers had begun establishing colonies in the Americas, and the leading colonial power in the sixteenth century was Spain. England understood the benefits of limiting Spanish influence in the New World, and sought to neutralize any economic advantages that Spain held. New colonies were established in North America and the Caribbean; these settlements also provided bases to launch attacks – often in league with the French and the Dutch – against Spanish ships carrying gold and silver. By the eighteenth century, the main rival in North America was France, and the British formed alliances with Native American nations in order to take control from the French.

Napoleon and beyond

The British use of the balance of power strategy blossomed in the early nineteenth century. This time the powerful threat was France, which – led by Napoleon – was taking control of large chunks of Europe. Napoleon's success reverberated through the rest of the continent. No single country was able to stop his string of military victories, although several large European powers shared an interest in seeing him defeated.

Great Britain – along with Prussia, Russia, Austria and Sweden – formed a series of **coalitions** to present a united front against Napoleon. It was the Fifth Coalition that finally achieved its aim when Napoleon's forces were defeated on 18 June 1815 at the Battle of Waterloo.

This practical application of the balance of power, achieved by alliances of different nations, would influence later thinking about how to conduct war, and maintain peace.

Over the course of the nineteenth century, more alliances evolved, split and even came to oppose each other. The drama was happening against a backdrop of **colonialism** as several of the European powers, notably Great Britain and France, were building empires based on trade. It was in their interests to preserve a balance of power on the home front within Europe, and they saw alliances as a way of doing that. Others, such as Germany, had only recently risen to power and needed foreign allies to sustain their gains. Out of this thinking arose the Triple Alliance of 1882, involving Germany, Austria-Hungary and Italy. This development alarmed Great Britain, France and Russia, who created a rival alliance known as the Triple Entente. Mistrust and anxiety spread through Europe, and it seemed that the tension would only be resolved through war.

A 19th century magistrate deals with local concerns during the time of the British Raj, or rule, over India.

HISTORY
World wars and world solutions

The basic outlines of the network of international co-operation evolved in the twentieth century. It was the harsh lessons of two global conflicts, which had ended millions of lives, which were behind efforts to create the new international **consensus**.

Inevitable outcome

The United Kingdom entered the twentieth century as a member of the Triple Entente (see page 7), which had begun as an agreement between France and Russia in the 1890s, and was expanded to include Great Britain between 1904 and 1907. Britain was bound to these other countries not by a firm **treaty** or **alliance**, but by a simple agreement to co-operate. Britain's aim, as usual, was to preserve European peace by maintaining the balance of power, but the other members were more closely involved with disputes that would prove to be the causes of the First World War. France was bitter after a military defeat by Germany in 1870–1, and Russia's interests clashed with Germany's in the Balkans.

It was this latter area that proved to be the trigger for war in 1914. In June 1914, a Serbian **nationalist** assassinated Archduke Franz Ferdinand of Austria-Hungary. Austria-Hungary declared war on Serbia, and because of complicated alliances, many other European countries were then drawn into war. Austria-Hungary, Germany, Turkey and some smaller countries were

pitched against the Allied Powers, led by Great Britain, France and Russia. Altogether, there were 32 countries involved in the war, including troops from the United States, Canada, Australia, New Zealand and India. This was war on a global scale: by the time the Allied powers achieved victory in November 1918, there were casualties to match. More than eight million soldiers had been killed, and about five million civilians also died as a result of the fighting.

The League of Nations

People were horrified by these losses and described the conflict as 'the war to end all wars'. The answer in preventing this sort of tragedy happening again seemed to lie in an international body that would act as a 'referee' between nations in dispute, forcing both sides to see reason. US President Woodrow Wilson proposed a plan for a general association of nations. This formed the basis of the League of Nations, which met for the first time on 15 November 1920, with 42 nations represented. Some 28 countries were members of the League of Nations throughout its existence. Another 35 either joined or withdrew during that time.

The League consisted of an assembly, a council, and a **secretariat** – a similar structure to today's United Nations (see pages 18–19). One of the most important aims of the League was to end the 'criminal threat of war'. In this respect it had some limited success. However, the Great Powers, such as Britain, France and Germany, chose to pursue their own foreign policies. This attitude, coupled with the fact that the United States never joined as a member, severely limited the League's power.

The Second World War

Britain, like other members of the League of Nations, would certainly have benefited from a prolonged period of peace, especially in the 1930s. The industrialized world felt the full effects of an economic depression at that time. Economic productivity declined as unemployment soared.

Similar economic conditions helped open a road to power for far-right political leaders, such as Adolf Hitler in Germany and Benito Mussolini in Italy. The gradual increase in their military power went unchecked by the League of Nations. By the late 1930s, the world seemed poised to enter another huge conflict.

The Second World War started in September 1939 when Germany's desire to expand its borders led it to invade Poland. The war raged for six years, with fighting on three continents. The scale of the Second World War cruelly dashed the hope that the First World War 'would end all wars'. Overall, more than 25 million soldiers and 30 million civilians died in the war.

The German dictator Adolf Hitler tried to use the 1936 Olympic Games in Berlin as a showcase for his Nazi regime.

HISTORY
A framework for peace

The death toll from the Second World War was upsetting enough, but by the end of the conflict it became apparent that this war had taken fighting in new and terrifying directions. It soon emerged that the Nazi government of Germany had systematically killed up to six million Jews, gypsies, homosexuals and others whom they deemed to be 'subhuman'. This wide scale slaughter, now referred to as the Holocaust, was almost beyond understanding. Furthermore, as American forces pushed steadily against the stubborn Japanese defences in 1945, US President Harry S. Truman decided to use newly developed atomic weapons to speed up the Japanese surrender. The effect of the two atomic bombs – dropped on the Japanese cities of Hiroshima and Nagasaki – did bring the war to a close, but with human suffering of nightmarish proportions.

The fresh experience of 'total war' (with widespread civilian casualties), coupled with a dawning realization of the enormous power of atomic weapons, helped renew efforts to provide an international framework for peace and economic cooperation. Some of the planning even took place during the war itself, following on from strategic conferences held by the 'Big Three' – US President Franklin Roosevelt, British Prime Minister Winston Churchill and Soviet Premier Joseph Stalin. In April 1945, representatives from 50

countries met in San Francisco to create the **charter** of the organization that would be called the United Nations (UN). The United Kingdom was one of the countries that signed this charter, which aimed – among other things – 'to maintain international peace and security'.

There were similar moves to help countries in Europe and elsewhere rebuild after the war. A 1944 conference in Bretton Woods, New Hampshire (USA) established the International Bank for Reconstruction and Development (also known as the World Bank) and a related institution, the International Monetary Fund (IMF), both of which aimed to help devastated countries.

The Cold War

Despite the wartime **alliance** with the Soviet Union and the birth of new international organizations, a great divide (fuelled by mistrust and fear of further conflict) developed between the Soviet Union and its Communist allies on the one hand, and the United States and its anti-Communist allies on the other. The Soviet Union had seen the most casualties in the Second World War, and in the years following the war it helped Communist regimes to establish themselves in a number of East European countries. These Communist allies, known negatively as **'satellites'** in the West, would provide a shield against future attacks on the Soviet

Union from the West. The United States, the UK and other Western countries viewed the creation of these alliances as the first stages in a Communist advance. Their fears increased when Mao Zedong established a Communist government in China in 1949. This international division between Communist and anti-Communist governments (also known as 'free market' governments) came to be known as the Cold War. The big powers on each side shied away from entering into actual armed conflict, but over the next four decades they used smaller, less powerful countries as battlegrounds to increase their own influence. The Cold War also brought in yet another era of military alliances. The UK helped form the North Atlantic Treaty Organization (NATO) in 1949; the Communist countries of Eastern Europe responded by forming the Warsaw Pact in 1955.

The division also spawned rival organizations to promote economic cooperation. In addition to participating in the World Bank and the IMF, the United States operated the Marshall Plan (1947–51) to help Western European countries rebuild their economies. The Communist response – which was necessary since these countries played no part in either the World Bank or the IMF – was the Council for Mutual Economic Assistance (Comecon), formed in 1949.

FIND OUT...

The Cold War played an important part in shaping the institutions and attitudes of the world community. To research this period in more detail, visit the Cold War Museum at www.coldwar.org

Representatives from 44 countries attended the 1944 Bretton Woods Conference, which saw the formation of the World Bank and the IMF.

PART 3

BRITAIN AND THE WORLD
Britain – an international community?

A combination of geography and history make the United Kingdom unique among European nations, and in many ways an international community in its own right. With the main island of Great Britain at its heart, the United Kingdom maintains a certain difference in relation to other European countries. A sense of individuality has been created on many levels, not least that of defence. It is important to state that Britain has not been successfully invaded since 1066 and the Norman Conquest. Naval threats from the Dutch, French and Spanish have been fought off through a combination of skilful sailors and favourable wind conditions. More recently, Britain withstood prolonged aerial attacks from the Germans during the Second World War (1939–45). In addition, Great Britain has thought of itself as the 'guardian' of Western Europe on two occasions: as the leading power aiming to control Napoleon in the early 1800s, and again during the first years of the Second World War.

The sense of individuality can take on another element – one of superiority. The British cherish their sense of fair play, Parliamentary **democracy**, an impartial legal system and unwritten **constitution**. Over the centuries, the British have looked across the narrow gap of the Channel and compared their own system with those that exist on the Continent – and have found the Continent lacking. This sense of suspicion is still an important theme running through British thinking at every level, from **Europhobe** organizations to **tabloid** headlines screaming 'Hop off you Frogs'.

Island communities

The identity – and even essence – of the United Kingdom is not **homogeneous**. Being different from the rest of Europe has not been enough to define 'Britishness'. Even the name United Kingdom is a clue to the fact that the nation as a whole is made up of different countries. The full term is 'the United Kingdom of Great Britain and Northern Ireland' (simply 'Ireland' until 1922). The 'core' elements of Britishness are those of the four nations – England, Scotland, Wales and Northern Ireland. And since the Labour party's election victory in 1997, Scotland, Wales and Northern Ireland have been given a greater say in how they govern themselves. By allowing these nations more freedom, the government argues, the United Kingdom's essential unity is best preserved.

But these groups are not the only elements that help make the United Kingdom a vibrant and varied culture. Britain's **imperial** legacy, carried on to some extent with the **Commonwealth** (see pages 22–23), accounts for the flow of **immigrants** into the country in the decades after the Second World War. New arrivals – especially from the West Indies and Asia – settled in Britain, and their children and grandchildren have helped to widen the idea of what it means to be British in a modern, multi-racial society.

The 'Irish question' has been a constant concern for the British for centuries, some would say back to the time when Norman soldiers from England first entered Ireland. More recently, the question has centred on the concept of Irish **self-determination** or independence. And understanding how the 'question' has been answered could shed light on how the UK can deal with other nations in the international arena, especially its nearest neighbours in Europe.

Ireland, of course, is Britain's nearest neighbour. Despite centuries of ill-feeling between the two countries, there is a strong core of common ground between them. Irish immigrants helped Britain develop during the **Industrial Revolution**, and there are centuries of shared history. The 26 counties of the Irish Republic became fully independent – and left the Commonwealth – in 1948, but relations with the UK have become warmer over time. This developing relationship underpinned the 1998 Good Friday Agreement, which has determined how the six counties of Northern Ireland would be governed.

FIND OUT...

To see how devolution works in the different nations of the UK, visit these web sites:
The Welsh National Assembly – www.wales.gov.uk
The Scottish Parliament – www.scottish.parl.uk
The Northern Ireland Assembly – www.ni-assembly.gov.uk

Left: The sizeable Bengali community in East London celebrates a Bengali festival, demonstrating the cultural diversity of the capital.

BRITAIN AND THE WORLD
The Foreign and Commonwealth Office

The Foreign and **Commonwealth** Office (FCO) is the government department that is solely concerned with the UK's international relations. It is the FCO that oversees UK **diplomatic** missions, and it actively encourages increased trade and cultural links. Through its involvement with the Commonwealth itself, the BBC World Service and the British Council, the FCO acts as the umbrella organization in representing Britain's interests. And although its specific tasks – and even its name – have evolved over time, the FCO has been performing this function for more than five centuries.

How the FCO operates

The mission of the Foreign and Commonwealth Office is 'to promote the national interests of the United Kingdom and to contribute to a strong world community'. The Secretary of State for Foreign and Commonwealth Affairs (the Foreign Secretary) is responsible to Parliament for the work of the FCO. He or she is supported by three Ministers of State and a Parliamentary Under-Secretary of State. The Permanent Under-Secretary (PUS) of the FCO, who is also Head of the Diplomatic Service, is responsible for giving advice to the Foreign Secretary on all aspects of foreign policy, and for the management of the FCO and Diplomatic Service. With the help of the Deputy Under-

Secretaries (DUSs), he or she supervises and coordinates the work of the Directors, who are responsible for the creation of policy and making full use of resources within their area of command.

These commands, or main subject areas, fall into three categories: geographical (for example, Europe, Africa and Commonwealth), functional (for example, International Security, Overseas Trade) and administrative (for example, Resources, Personnel and Security). Legal and economic advisers and other departments provide specialist advice to Ministers and FCO departments.

Cabinet-level dilemmas

The FCO's Departmental Report, published in April, sets out its objectives and achievements over the past year, highlighting the progress the department has made in achieving the Government's foreign policy goals. For example, Robin Cook, Foreign Secretary between 1997 and 2001, aimed to operate an '**ethical** foreign policy'. This aim, which needed the approval of the **Cabinet**, was difficult to put into practice. During the full term of Parliament following Labour's 1997 victory, Cook found himself faced with some difficult decisions, mainly because the aim of an ethical foreign policy sometimes clashed with his Cabinet brief to promote national interests. The sale of warplanes to

Indonesia was one example. Selling Indonesia these planes (which provided Britain with jobs and millions of pounds) meant that the Indonesian government was better equipped to pursue aggressive (and internationally condemned) action against islanders on East Timor.

Similar dilemmas can sometimes create bad relations within the Cabinet itself. The Foreign Minister is very much in the 'front line', being the leading spokesman on British interests in various international and regional organizations. There is always the danger that things can go wrong. For example, one of the main reasons that Margaret Thatcher was forced out of her position as Conservative leader and Prime Minister in 1990 was because she disagreed with her more pro-European Foreign Minister, Geoffrey Howe.

FIND OUT...

It tends to be the treaties and protocols signed by the Foreign Secretary that make headlines, but the FCO is constantly preparing policy papers for distribution nationally and internationally. Typical of these is 'Focus International', a series of papers intended to provide accurate and balanced information on topics of current international interest. Their scope is wide-ranging and includes:

>> topics currently on the international agenda, such as international conferences
>> areas of conflict and human rights abuses in certain countries
>> issues of wide and long-term interest, including the environment, world trade, development issues and drug trafficking.

Distributed throughout the world, 'Focus International' papers are particularly useful in circumstances where there are few local resources for research. Some 'Focus International' papers are translated into other languages. You can access them on the Foreign Office's website at www.fco.gov.uk

UK Prime Minister Tony Blair, with the then Foreign Secretary Robin Cook, prepares the UK contribution to the European Union summit in Nice in December 2000.

BRITAIN AND THE WORLD
New neighbours – the European Union

Millions of Britons take holidays in Europe each year. Regular television broadcasts keep British viewers informed about sporting events such as the many top-class athletics championships staged across the Continent. Britain's total trade with its European partners – both in imports and exports – continues to rise year on year. Yet 'Europe' remains a controversial issue for the main British political parties. We constantly hear slogans which contradict each other, such as 'within Europe but not ruled by Europe' and 'a stronger Britain within a wider Europe', and countless headlines mock what is often seen as the biggest 'threat' of all – Brussels, headquarters of the European Union (EU).

What is the EU?

The EU is the result of a process of cooperation and **integration**, which began in 1951 between six countries. After fifty years and four waves of **accessions**, the EU now has fifteen member states and is preparing for more to join. The EU name came into use on 1 November 1993, after the three main strands of European cooperation were brought together: the European Community (including the **single market** and single currency), the Common Foreign and Security Policy (CFSP) and the area of Justice and Home Affairs (JHA) cooperation.

The EU headquarters in Brussels will need to accommodate representatives of more member states if plans for EU expansion are agreed.

Within the European Community, the member governments act as the Council (often taking decisions by **majority vote**). CFSP and JHA decisions are based on intergovernmental processes. This means that member states act together to reach a joint position based on **consensus**. Other Community institutions, such as the European Commission and the European Parliament, have a more limited role. Intergovernmental Conferences (IGCs) create and amend the **treaties** upon which the EU is based.

Britain's involvement

In March 1957, the foreign ministers of the six Continental nations formulated the two Treaties of Rome, which created the European Economic Community (EEC), the forerunner of the EU. In response to the EEC, Great Britain and six other non-EEC countries formed the European Free Trade Association (EFTA) in 1960. But it soon became clear that the British economy was growing less rapidly than those of the EEC members. In 1961, Prime Minister Harold Macmillan applied for British membership of the EEC, but President Charles de Gaulle of France blocked the application.

In 1973, Prime Minister Edward Heath, an important pro-European, led the UK's admission to the EEC. Two years later the first national **referendum** in British history approved the step by a margin of two votes to one. In the years since then, the UK relationship with the EU has been volatile – occasionally Britain will cooperate with the EU, but more often it has rejected or weakened measures aimed at increasing European unity.

Money – the real issue?

Just as the EU has taken on the role of a 'regional United Nations', preserving the interests of Europe as a whole to safeguard the interests of individual member states, it has also begun playing a greater role in using finance as a means of promoting cooperation. The issue that has grabbed the British headlines, of course, is that of the Single European Currency (Euro), which has begun gradually replacing individual currencies (notably the German Deutschmark, French Franc and the Italian Lira) in participating countries.

Reflecting the aims and practices of the World Bank (see pages 10–11), the European Union has its own financing institution – the European Investment Bank (EIB). The EIB's mission is to further the objectives of the European Union by providing long-term finance for specific projects in keeping with strict banking practice. Britain's nearest neighbour, the Republic of Ireland, has financed much of its recent development with EIB funds.

FIND OUT...

The European Union has a web site that covers all aspects of its work and institutions.
Visit it at www.europa.eu.int

A WORLD FRAMEWORK
The United Nations

The United Nations is an important international body. As one of the founding members of the League of Nations (see pages 8–9), the UK was well placed to learn from past mistakes, and so it has played an important part in the work of the United Nations since it began in 1945.

Laying the groundwork

The United Kingdom was one of the 'Big Three' group of allies during the Second World War (along with the United States and the Soviet Union). The leaders of these countries set the basis for a future international organization aimed at promoting peace and cooperation. Britain varied its traditional 'balance of power' strategy by ensuring that the two potential enemies were members from the outset. On 30 October 1943, at a conference in Moscow, representatives of the Soviet Union, Great Britain, China and the United States signed a declaration in which they recognized the need to establish 'at the earliest practicable date a general international organization'. Meeting in Teheran, Iran, a month later, Winston Churchill, Franklin Roosevelt and Soviet Premier Joseph Stalin spoke of 'the supreme responsibility resting upon us and all the United Nations to make a peace which will … banish the scourge and terror of war'.

A framework for peace

Just two months after the Second World War ended, representatives from 50 countries established a **charter** that turned the United Nations (UN) from an idea into reality. These 'peace-loving states' (in the words of the charter) also set about building the UN structure that we know today. The United Nations is made up of six principal parts: the General Assembly, the Security Council, the Economic and Social Council, the Trusteeship Council, the International Court of Justice, and the **Secretariat**.

>> The General Assembly is its 'parliament', and all member states are represented in it. It meets annually in regular sessions, and in special sessions at the request of a majority of its members or of the Security Council. It makes recommendations to member states, but these cannot be enforced.

>> The Security Council is the UN's central organ for maintaining peace. It has fifteen members: five of these – the UK, China, France, Russia (occupying the seat of the former Soviet Union) and the United States – have permanent seats. Non-permanent members serve two-year terms, with five new members elected by the General Assembly every year. Council decisions require nine votes; however, any one of the five permanent members can **veto** a major

issue. If the Council believes that a dispute threatens peace, it can enforce its recommendations, either by non-military means, such as economic or **diplomatic sanctions**, or by the use of military force.

>> The Economic and Social Council (ECOSOC), which meets annually, has 54 members: 18 members are elected each year by the General Assembly for three-year terms. ECOSOC coordinates the economic and social activities of the UN. It studies international topics such as medicine and education, and recommends action on these.

>> The Trusteeship Council was set up to supervise 11 territories placed under international trust at the end of the Second World War. By the early 1990s all of the original trust territories had been dissolved.

>> The International Court of Justice, situated in The Hague, the Netherlands, is the **judicial** body of the UN. It hears cases referred to it by UN members, who hold the right to decide whether they will accept the court's ruling as final. Fifteen judges, elected for nine-year terms, sit as members of the court.

>> The Secretariat carries out the administrative tasks of the UN. It is headed by the Secretary General, who is appointed by the General Assembly on the recommendation of the Security Council. The Secretary General acts as the UN spokesperson.

FIND OUT...

Discover more about the institutions and history of the UN at www.un.org

Swedish Prime Minister Goran Persson addressing the UN Millennium Summit, September 2000.

A WORLD FRAMEWORK
The UN agencies

The United Kingdom has been a pioneer as well as an active member of the various specialized branches of the United Nations. Representatives of such agencies are the only point of contact that many people will ever have with the United Nations itself, so in many respects these officials act as 'UN ambassadors'.

Food and Agriculture Organization (FAO)

The goal of the FAO is to achieve freedom from hunger. The FAO is responsible for distributing information about nutrition, food and agriculture. It also supports measures to conserve natural resources, combat animal and plant diseases and to increase crop yields in areas of the world that are subject to famine.

World Health Organization (WHO)

The WHO, based at Geneva in Switzerland, was established in 1948 as a means of making 'the highest possible levels of health' available to everyone. It provides advice on a range of infectious diseases, family planning, nutrition and sanitation. 'On-the-scene' demonstrations of farming techniques and health care help develop better hygiene standards.

International Labour Organization (ILO)

The ILO aims to raise living standards by improving work conditions and promoting productive employment. The ILO existed before the UN itself, being established in 1919 as part of the League of Nations. It was officially linked to the UN in 1946.

UN peacekeeping

The UN Charter gives the responsibility of maintaining peace to the Security Council. Since the first UN peacekeeping mission in 1948, more than 100 nations have contributed military personnel at different times. The UK has been a strong supporter of these efforts, supplying troops and equipment during a number of conflicts, for example, during the Gulf War of 1991.

UN High Commission for Refugees (UNHCR)

One of the consequences of warfare and other conflicts has been the rise of refugees – people whose homes have been destroyed or whose lives are in danger in their homeland. The UNHCR provides field stations, base camps, temporary shelters and essential medical relief to such people.

UN Educational, Scientific and Cultural Organization (UNESCO)

UNESCO was created in 1946 to promote world peace by focusing on the areas of culture and communication, education and natural, social and human sciences.

UN Children's Fund (UNICEF)

The United Nations Children's Fund (UNICEF) focuses on long-term human development, although it also offers emergency relief and **rehabilitation** assistance when necessary. More than 130 countries receive UNICEF support for health care, nutrition, basic education, and water and sanitation programmes.

UN emergency relief at work – a plane arrives with 17 tonnes of food for Somalia's famine victims in the early 1990s.

UNDP

The United Nations Development Programme (UNDP), established by the General Assembly in 1965, works with some 150 governments and 30 intergovernmental agencies to provide technical assistance in improving living standards and promoting economic growth in the developing nations of Asia, Africa, Latin America, the Middle East and parts of Europe. More than 20,000 UN volunteers have worked in about 140 countries.

Keeping the peace

Although there has been no global war since the end of the Second World War in 1945, not a single day has gone by without fighting somewhere in the world. More people have died in the over 100 'small wars' that have taken place since the Second World War than died in the six years of fighting. Clearly, the United Nations peacekeeping efforts remain a vital concern for all UN member states.

WORLD FOOD

UN

A WORLD FRAMEWORK
The Commonwealth

While Britain may have 'lost an empire' (see pages 26–27), it has not lost its links with the dozens of countries stretched around the world which once coloured the world map pink (the traditional colour indicating the British Empire). Apart from a few small colonies and dependencies dotted across the globe, nearly all of these countries are now fully independent.

A shared background

Most of the newly independent countries wanted to preserve links with both the United Kingdom and with the other countries that had once formed part of the British Empire. The answer was to become members of the **Commonwealth** of Nations. The title 'Commonwealth of Nations' was first used officially at the Imperial Conference of 1926, referring to 'the group of self-governing communities composed of Great Britain and the Dominions'. This definition was embodied in the Statute of Westminster, which was made into law by the British Parliament in 1931. When India became a **republic** in 1949, it continued its membership in the Commonwealth, setting a precedent followed by many former British colonies.

The Commonwealth is an association of 54 independent member countries. These countries are found in North America, the Caribbean, Europe, the Mediterranean, Africa and Asia. They are also in the Atlantic, Indian and Pacific Oceans. The Commonwealth has its headquarters at Marlborough House in London. It elects a Commonwealth Secretary-General just as the United Nations chooses its own Secretary-General. The Commonwealth has no official policy-making body, and the only formal political consultations among the member governments are the regular meetings of their prime ministers to discuss common problems.

Strength in diversity

The relationship between countries of the Commonwealth resembles that of the United Nations, and the experience of dealing with each other in the friendlier context of the Commonwealth is a great advantage for many members. For example, the Commonwealth includes some of the world's biggest countries and some of its smallest. India, for example, has more than one billion people. The smallest countries are Nauru and Tuvalu in the Pacific Ocean, each with about 11,000 people. In the wider setting of the United Nations, similar small countries often find themselves without a voice. But their needs are expressed – and heard – more forcefully within the Commonwealth, and these concerns can then be passed on to wider audiences in the UN General Assembly.

One example – of great concern to both Nauru and Tuvalu – is the effect that global warming has had on sea levels. These countries are both low-lying island nations and even a small rise in sea level, caused by melting ice caps, would be devastating. This problem also affects other non-Commonwealth island countries, but they lack the sense of cooperation and mutual support that Commonwealth membership gives.

Likewise, the Commonwealth members are some of the world's richest countries and some of the poorest. Australia, Canada, Singapore and the United Kingdom are all among the leading nations in the world in terms of economic activity. Some of the poorest are Mozambique, Sierra Leone and Tanzania. Again, these poorer countries benefit from having a

chance to express their needs within a setting that is less confrontational than that of the United Nations.

The Commonwealth is packed with 'people power', and the statistics about how it is made up show that its role in the future may become even more persuasive on the world stage. Overall, there are 1.7 billion people in the Commonwealth. That staggering amount is more than one quarter (the exact figure is 29.8 per cent) of the total world population. And even more important is its age make-up. About half of the people in the Commonwealth are less than 25 years old. These are the people who will become the decision-makers of tomorrow.

Queen Elizabeth II and the Duke of Edinburgh are sheltered from the sun as they meet senior politicians in the West African Commonwealth country, Ghana.

A WORLD FRAMEWORK
Reaching out

In addition to being an enthusiastic member of the various UN agencies, the United Kingdom is at the forefront of dozens of international charities which, like the UN volunteers programme, operate in many countries experiencing problems in such areas as health, natural disasters, warfare and human rights abuses.

When the British Empire began to break down in the twentieth century, British people were at the forefront of many volunteer agencies, which supplement the work of 'official' agencies under the 'protection' of the United Nations or regional bodies. Some of these agencies, such as Oxfam and Amnesty International, have become major international organizations in their own right, attracting volunteers from dozens of other countries.

These pages take a close look at a few of these organizations, examining their structures, aims and ideals.

Voluntary Service Overseas (VSO) is an international development charity that works through volunteers. It enables people aged 17–70 to share their skills and experience with local communities in the developing world.

The approach is successful and popular. VSO is the largest independent volunteer-sending agency in the world. Since 1958, it has sent out more than 29,000 volunteers to work in Africa, Asia, the Pacific region and, recently, Eastern Europe in response to requests from its overseas partners. At any one time there are about 2,000 people engaged on placements in these regions.

Making food a priority

One of the most respected international aid agencies is Oxfam, which has been operating for more than half a century. It takes its name from the Oxford Committee for Famine Relief, which first met in October 1942 to address the problems of famine in Greece. During the Second World War, the Nazis occupied Greece. After the war, the Committee (which gradually became known by its abbreviated name – Oxfam) concentrated on supplying food parcels and clothing to the parts of Europe that were still suffering. In 1949, the Committee's objectives were again broadened to include 'the relief of suffering arising as a result of wars or of other causes in any part of the world.'

Remembering the forgotten

Peter Benenson, a British lawyer, launched Amnesty International in 1961 after he read about two Portuguese students who had been sentenced to seven years' imprisonment for raising their glasses in a toast to freedom. His newspaper appeal, 'The Forgotten Prisoners', was published worldwide on 28 May 1961, and brought in more than 1,000 offers of support for the idea of an international campaign to protect human rights. Within twelve months the new organization had sent representatives to four countries to make pleas on behalf of prisoners, had taken up 210 cases and had

Amnesty International spokesman, Geoffrey Binderman, with a photographic display of 'the disappeared', probable victims of the Pinochet regime in Chile in the 1970s and 1980s.

organized national branches in seven countries. The process has continued and today's Amnesty members work by the same principles of strict impartiality (not favouring one side more than another) and independence that has guided the organization from the start.

Campaigning for children

Save the Children was created in 1919. It has become one of the leading international campaigning organizations for the rights of children. Working from the fact that more children now are born into poverty and suffer from war and natural disasters than at any other time in modern history, Save the Children is involved in a wide range of campaigns, **lobbying** bodies such as the United Nations, and promoting programmes in education, health care, environmentally sound agriculture and economic productivity that are appropriate to the area involved.

FIND OUT...

'Ours is a very individual "people to people" approach to development. Our overriding goal is to help individuals learn from each other – and consequently benefit the communities and countries in which they live. But above all, we are realistic in our expectations. We purposefully harness our resources to long-term objectives and focus on sustainable development rather than the short-term relief of certain problems.'

This is VSO official policy, as outlined on their website. You can find it at www.vso.org.uk

A WORLD FRAMEWORK
Economic matters

It is often said that people 'vote with their purses'. This basic analysis of voters' intentions is recognized by political leaders – governments often propose new tax cuts or payment schemes just before an election – and it also shows how economic matters are at the heart of the **democratic** process. The ability to be '**fiscally** prudent', while still providing essential services and public spending, is the goal of most Chancellors of the Exchequer in Britain and their counterparts in other countries.

Similarly, foreign policy is often affected, or even led, by financial concerns. Critics of the Gulf War in 1991 argued that a **coalition** of military powers would never have been created if Kuwait had not had important oil reserves. Nevertheless, the stated aim of most countries is to provide and maintain a network of international trade. A number of interconnected organizations and agreements support this aim, and the United Kingdom plays an important role in all of them.

Restoring order

At the end of the Second World War, senior economists were trying to guarantee an international framework of financial security. In July 1944, representatives from 44 nations attended the United Nations Monetary and Financial Conference at Bretton Woods, in New Hampshire, USA. The 'Bretton Woods Conference' led to the creation of two powerful financial institutions: the International Monetary Fund (IMF) and the International Bank for Reconstruction and Development (commonly known as the World Bank). In the years immediately following the Second World War, both institutions concentrated on rebuilding European economies that had suffered during the war; in later years both the IMF and the World Bank have taken on a more international role in encouraging and monitoring economic development in the **Third World**.

The World Bank

The International Bank for Reconstruction and Development (World Bank) is a specialized UN agency that was set up at the same time as the IMF. The **charter** of the bank indicates that it aims to promote development among its member countries. The bank grants loans only to member nations, which must use the money for specific projects. Before a nation can secure a loan, World Bank advisers must determine that the prospective borrower can meet conditions set out by the bank. World Bank members must already belong to the IMF, so the two organizations are often seen as working together. Like the IMF, the World Bank has faced its share of criticism, particularly from the 1960s onwards, as it gave more emphasis to developing countries. Many observers believed that the World Bank favoured large-scale schemes (such as hydroelectric dams) that can harm the environment.

Responding to these concerns, the World Bank has given more attention to projects that could directly benefit the poorest people in developing nations, by helping them to raise their productivity and to gain access to safe water and waste-disposal facilities, health care, family-planning assistance, nutrition, education and housing. Direct involvement of the poorest people in economic activity has been promoted by providing loans for agriculture and rural development, small-scale enterprises and urban development.

British Chancellor of the Exchequer, Gordon Brown, greets the Ugandan Secretary to the Treasury soon after announcing the UK government's pledge to write off £56 million of debts owed by devoloping countries.

International Monetary Fund

The IMF, which began in 1947, is a specialized agency of the United Nations, made up of 183 member-nations. It aims to promote international **monetary** cooperation so that international trade can grow. The IMF targets **exchange rate** stability and orderly exchange arrangements as core issues. These help it to increase economic growth and levels of employment, and to provide temporary financial assistance to countries to help ease **balance of payments** problems.

Members agree to keep the IMF informed about economic and financial policies that affect the exchange value of their national currencies, so that other members can make appropriate decisions based on these policies. On joining the fund, each member is assigned a **quota** in special drawing rights (SDRs), the fund's unit of currency. The value of SDRs is based on the average value of five major currencies, including the pound sterling. Each member's quota is an amount corresponding to its position in the world economy. The United Kingdom is one of the key players within the IMF. Its major role in the world economy ensures that it has one of the highest quotas of SDRs.

However, the IMF is sometimes accused of 'playing politics'. Some smaller countries argue that the Fund forces them to adopt difficult economic policies to meet the demands of larger countries (including the UK). British governments have had to face tough criticism at home and abroad after some of its financial decisions have affected members of the **Commonwealth**.

A WORLD FRAMEWORK
Wider responsibilities

The United Kingdom is a key player in many other international trading frameworks, several of which work alongside (or within) what is described as the 'Bretton Woods framework' – the series of agreements that formed the World Bank, the International Monetary Fund and their associated bodies. Several of these other organizations – notably the OECD and G8 - have been described as 'rich men's clubs' because countries with the most powerful economies dominate their membership.

The OECD

The Organization for Economic Cooperation and Development (OECD) describes itself as 'a club of 30 like-minded member countries'. These countries are among the world's most powerful in economic terms, so it is not surprising that the OECD is seen by some as the preserve of the rich.

The core of original members has expanded from Europe and North America to include Japan, Australia, New Zealand, Finland, Mexico, the Czech Republic, Hungary, Poland and South Korea.

George W. Bush chose the UK Prime Minister Tony Blair as the first European leader to meet after his election. Their relationship has become even more important since the terrorist attacks on the United States on 11 September 2001 (see page 33).

Some OECD discussion and debate has led to formal agreements – for example, by establishing agreements to crack down on bribery or to end **subsidies** for shipbuilding. Increasingly, though, the OECD is engaging in cross-studies that bring together the work of specialists in different sectors. Environment and economic analysis can no longer be examined in isolation; trade and investment are inextricably linked.

G8 and beyond

If the OECD finds it important to dispel the 'rich man image', then the Group of Eight (G8) sits at the opposite end of the publicity spectrum. This group, which was originally called G7, began with meetings of representatives of the United States, Japan, the United Kingdom, West Germany, France, Italy and Canada - the seven most powerful economies. It rose to eight with the inclusion of Russia. These countries are the real 'movers and shakers' in the world economy and any **consensus** among them would have wide-ranging effects across the globe.

GATT and the WTO

The General Agreement on **Tariffs** and Trade (GATT) was a **treaty** and international trade organization that lasted from 1948 to 1995. GATT members worked to minimize tariffs, **quotas**, and **preferential trade agreements** between countries and other barriers to international trade.

In 1995, GATT's functions were taken over by the World Trade Organization (WTO), an international body that organizes trade laws and provides a forum for settling trade disputes among nations.

The World Trade Organization (WTO) describes itself as 'the only global international organization dealing with the rules of trade between nations'. At its heart are the WTO agreements, negotiated and signed by the bulk of the world's trading nations and established in their parliaments. The goal is to help producers of goods and services, exporters, and importers to conduct their businesses.

WTO meetings are often disrupted by protesters who feel that the decisions made are for the benefit of wealthy countries and big business. The protesters represent a number of different interests, and can be:

>> **Lobbyists** on behalf of the developing countries who feel that the WTO represents the richer nations

>> Environmental protesters who feel that the interests of big business are directly opposed to protecting our environment

>> Trade unionists who believe that global companies will use cheap labour in developing countries to cut costs, causing workers in the richer nations to lose their jobs

>> **Anarchists** who oppose any regulation of world trade.

A WORLD FRAMEWORK
Military and security co-operation

Every nation must be prepared to pursue its foreign policy through military means if all the **diplomatic** channels have been exhausted. The United Kingdom is no exception. It was Britain's military power, particularly the Royal Navy, which has both protected the British Empire and allowed it to expand. The old military policy of trying to increase a country's territory is no longer acceptable in the current climate of international agreements created by the United Nations and other multinational bodies. But that does not rule out the need for a strong military. Even now, in the era of the 'peace dividend' (the term used to describe the lessening of tension as a result of the end of the Cold War), the military is an integral part of British life.

The role of the military at the beginning of the twenty-first century, however, is very different to the way things were at the beginning of the twentieth century. With the two world wars now history, and with the **arms race** linked to the Cold War also over, military **alliances** now play a genuine peace-keeping role. The United Kingdom is a team player in several such alliances, notably within the North Atlantic **Treaty** Organization (NATO) and as an enthusiastic participant in a number of UN peacekeeping ventures.

NATO composition

NATO is a regional defence alliance, created by the North Atlantic Treaty, which was signed on 4 April 1949. The original countries to sign the Treaty were Belgium, Canada, Denmark, France, Iceland, Italy, Luxembourg, the Netherlands, Norway, Portugal, the United Kingdom and the United States. Greece and Turkey were admitted to the alliance in 1952, West Germany in 1955 and Spain in 1982. NATO aims to promote the stability, well-being, and freedom of its members through a system of collective security. In 1990, the newly unified Germany replaced West Germany as a NATO member.

The highest authority within NATO is the North Atlantic Council, which is composed of permanent delegates from all member countries, headed by a Secretary General. As the decision-making body of NATO, it is responsible for general policy and administration. Several committees, notably the **Secretariat** and the Military Committee, report to the North Atlantic Council. The Secretary General runs the Secretariat, which handles all the non-military functions of the alliance. The Military Committee, which meets twice a year, consists of the chiefs of staff of the various armed forces. Below the Military Committee are the various geographical commands: Allied Command Europe, Allied Command Atlantic, Allied Command Channel, and the Regional Planning Group (for North America). These commands are in charge of making use of armed forces in their areas.

Another watchdog

NATO is backed up by another organization that is focused on Europe – the Organization for Security and Co-operation in Europe (OSCE). This regional security organization has 55 participating states (including the UK) from Europe, Central Asia and North America. The OSCE has been established as the body that will deal with the prevention of conflict, crisis management and post-conflict **rehabilitation** under Chapter VIII of the **Charter** of the United Nations.

The OSCE approach to security addresses a wide range of security-related issues including arms control, preventive diplomacy, confidence- and security-building measures, human rights, election monitoring and economic and environmental security. All OSCE participating states have equal status, and decisions are based on **consensus**. The OSCE works in specific areas to progress political processes, prevent or settle conflicts, and inform the OSCE community. The largest field activity is the OSCE Mission in Kosovo, with more than 2100 staff. OSCE field activities are established by Permanent Council Decision with agreement by the host country.

For decades, NATO troops practised military exercises to prepare for a possible nuclear or conventional attack from the Soviet Union and its allies. Its role changed dramatically in the 1990s, following the breakdown of the Communist system in Russia and the violent collapse of the former Yugoslavia. The threat of another world war seemed to have passed, but UK troops (under NATO direction) became involved in the conflicts in Bosnia and later in Kosovo, a disputed region of Serbia.

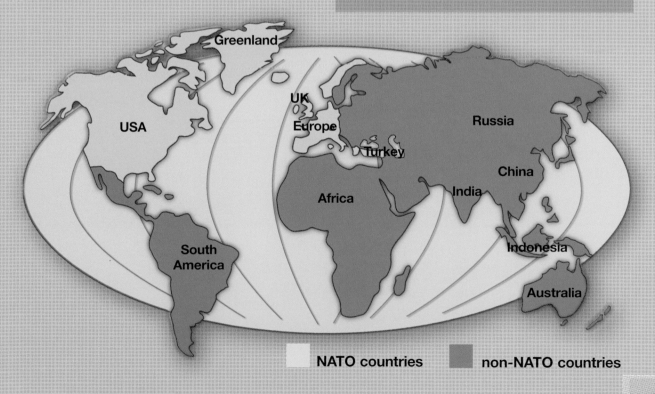

Greenland · USA · UK · Europe · Turkey · Russia · China · India · Africa · South America · Indonesia · Australia

☐ **NATO countries**   ☐ **non-NATO countries**

A WORLD FRAMEWORK
Working for peace

Governments that have volunteered the use of their troops for UN peacekeeping missions keep command of their soldiers. British soldiers – at present involved in UN missions in Bosnia, Cyprus, the Democratic Republic of Congo, East Timor, Georgia, the Iraq-Kuwait border, Kosovo and Sierra Leone – wear their normal uniforms, but they also wear distinctive blue berets or helmets with the UN logo.

The presence of UN peacekeeping forces is often enough to calm things down, and the UN forces are generally only lightly armed for self-defence. Sometimes, though, their weapons must be used and soldiers are injured or killed. Since 1948, about 1600 UN military and civilian personnel have died whilst performing their duties.

Apart from their military role, UN peacekeepers carry out a number of political, medical and **humanitarian** activities as part of their mission. Election observers, medical staff and human rights monitors work alongside the soldiers in many cases. Their job is to help an area return to normal, so that ultimately, it has free elections and human rights. In the meantime, they must try to make a place safe for its inhabitants by finding temporary housing for refugees, clearing landmines and training police forces to maintain order.

Other channels for peace

Military and security **alliances** such as NATO grew out of the tension of the Cold War period. Officials at government level agreed that collective security was the only defence against the threat posed by the Soviet Union and its Communist allies. Those same tensions, however, provoked very different responses among many ordinary people who felt that the best answer to the threat of war is to *reduce* the amount of weapons on both sides, rather than trying to achieve a balance or outdo the enemy.

Out of this concern grew a number of campaigning groups within the United Kingdom and beyond. The most famous of these organizations is the Campaign for Nuclear Disarmament (CND), which began a quest to raise public awareness about the dangers and expense of nuclear weapons during the 1950s. CND marches and demonstrations kept the issue of nuclear war in the public eye during the Cold War, and the organization still campaigns for a reduction in these weapons.

Playing a similar role is the International Campaign to Ban Landmines (ICBL), which Diana, Princess of Wales did much to publicize. The ICBL concentrates its efforts on ridding the world of landmines, weapons that wound and kill hundreds of innocent people each year – even years after conflicts have ended. ICBL was awarded the Nobel Peace Prize in 1997.

Keeping the peace in Sierra Leone

In May 2000, UN Secretary General Kofi Annan stated that several of the guiding principles behind UN peacekeeping needed to be rethought. Rebel leaders in Sierra Leone had held more than 100 peacekeepers hostage, and the force lacked the firepower or authority to impose order on the troubled country. Annan argued that UN missions should have more weapons and wider powers to enforce a settlement in such circumstances, and that there should be a time when UN peacekeepers abandon their neutral position. Many of today's conflicts are started by unofficial military leaders who will only respond to firm military action, rather than peacekeeping and negotiation.

The first war of the new century

Despite the end of the Cold War and the increased friendliness between former opponents, it seemed likely that any new, large-scale conflict would not follow the 'rules' that had previously applied. The terrible attacks on New York City and Washington D.C. on 11 September 2001 gave the world a chilling example of what was possible. Nearly 5000 people died in the terrorist attacks that day, and the world waited to see how the remaining superpower would react. Within the week, UK Prime Minister Tony Blair had declared that Britain, like the United States, was 'at war with terrorism'. Others countries pledged their support, and NATO (see pages 30–31) declared the attack on the United States to be the same as an attack on all its member countries.

After a month of negotiations and preparation, the US and British forces launched into raids on Taleban-controlled Afghanistan, headquarters of the al-Qa'ida terrorist network and its leader, Saudi exile Osama bin Laden. Around the world sympathy for the Americans continued, but there were also many questioning the need to fight terrorism with yet more death and destruction.

These people in the Philippines show their opposition to the terrorist attack on the United States, but also oppose a military response.

A WORLD FRAMEWORK
Justice for all?

In many ways, it is easiest to understand the complex network of international organizations by thinking of the world as one unit (comparable to a country) and considering the organizations as being like the different branches of government in a single country. Organizations such as the UN General Assembly and the European Parliament echo the **legislative** branch of national government – Parliament, in the case of the United Kingdom. Likewise, UN peacekeeping ventures, plus international security **alliances** such as NATO, resemble a sort of international Ministry of Defence. Even the **executive** branch of government – the role played by the US President – has its equivalent in positions such as the EU presidency, which 'rotates' among EU member states.

The missing branch

The remaining government 'ministry' that needs an international counterpart, of course, is the **judiciary**. That role is played by the International Court of Justice (or 'World Court'). This was created in 1945 under the UN Charter as the successor to the Permanent Court of International Justice under the League of Nations. The court decides legal cases between nations; individuals may not bring cases before the court. All members of the UN are subject to the rule of the World Court.

Disputes are brought before the court in two ways. The first is by a special agreement, under which all parties agree to submit the matter to the court. The second is by a **unilateral** application by one party to the dispute. For example, in case of a dispute, a country might claim that its enemy is obliged by the terms of a

Belgrade readers learn of the arrest of former Yugoslavian President Slobodan Milosevic on 1 April 2001. He is to be tried by the UN War Crimes Tribunal.

particular **treaty** to accept the authority of the court. The UN Security Council has the power to take measures to enforce the decision of the court if the parties to the dispute fail to enforce it themselves. In practice, however, nations have been able to ignore World Court rulings.

Making things permanent

The international judicial organizations as they exist at present only exist to perform a specific function (such as dealing with the issue of war crimes in the former Yugoslavia). However, many observers have called for an International Court of Criminal Justice. Such a court would have a permanent staff, and cases could be heard far more quickly because it would not need special UN legislation to set things moving.

But there has also been strong criticism of these suggestions. Sir Norman Lamont, who was Chancellor of the Exchequer under Conservative Prime Minister John Major, points out that such a permanent institution would 'hold Britain (and other powerful nations) hostage' to the whims of smaller nations with grievances. Without the electoral authority, such as the power of **veto** in the UN Security Council, the UK would be forced to defend itself against, for example Iraq, Afghanistan or any other regime that the UK deems to be a threat. These arguments for and against have been echoed in many other countries, and it remains to be seen whether any type of permanent international court will take shape in the foreseeable future.

War crimes

The international community sometimes agrees that the behaviour of some military personnel goes beyond accepted conduct in wartime. In such instances, special courts (or tribunals) hear the cases. The first time this type of justice was used was in the series of trials in Nuremberg, Germany, in the years following the Second World War. In a series of highly publicized trials, senior Nazi officials were tried – and some executed – for their behaviour against Jews, gypsies and others in prison camps.

More recently, dozens of Bosnian, Serbian, Croatian and other soldiers in the former Yugoslavia have been held and tried by the International Criminal Tribunal for the Former Yugoslavia. Documents known as 'Rule 61 Proceedings' are issued against suspects, and it is the responsibility of governments to hand these individuals over to the tribunal, based at The Hague in the Netherlands. The tribunal has compiled two million pages of documents, 3000 videos and thousands of tapes as evidence. One of the most important of its suspects, Slobodan Milosevic (the former leader of Serbia), was arrested in the spring of 2001. Later in the year, the Serbian government handed him over to the war crimes tribunal.

BUILDING A WORLD COMMUNITY
Operating on all levels

It would be impossible, in a book of this size, to list every international organization of which the United Kingdom is a member. Even within the categories dealt with here – **legislative** groups such as the United Nations, military **alliances** such as NATO and **judicial** bodies such as the World Court – there are others pursuing similar goals. But there are many areas where Britain's membership in world organizations plays an important part. These range from sporting and cultural groups to scientific associations, and also include many important **treaties** and **protocols** designed, for example, to protect the environment. Here, we will look at some examples and examine their aims and achievements.

Science and the environment

>> The British Antarctic Survey is responsible for all of the British Government's scientific research in the Antarctic, South Georgia and the South Sandwich Islands. The Survey began in 1943 as a wartime naval operation. Between August and November, BAS works with the World Meteorological Organization (WMO) to release regular bulletins on the state of the ozone layer. WMO combines information from stations on earth and space-based reports in these bulletins. Some of the data comes from orbiting satellites launched by the European Space Agency (ESA), of which the UK is a prominent member.

>> The United Nations Convention on the Law of the Sea came into being on 16 November 1994, after lengthy discussions by more than 150 countries representing all regions of the world. The Convention embodies the notion that all ocean-related problems are closely inter-related and need to be addressed as a whole. Today, the Convention is the globally recognized body that deals with all matters relating to the law of the sea.

Raw materials and commodities

Many of the world's products are produced or gathered in developing countries, which often have little say in the big trading organizations such as the OECD and WTO. To make matters worse, most consumers of these commodities are the very countries that do tend to dictate terms in such organizations. As a result, there are many trading agreements dealing with the production and trade of single products, to try to ensure that both producers and consumers get a fair deal. The International Coffee Organization (ICO) is one such body. It is an intergovernmental organization of 62 member countries serving the international coffee community. Established in 1963, the ICO brings producing and consuming countries together to exchange views and debate policy issues.

An important trading area in which the United Kingdom stands outside of an international agreement is in the field of oil and petroleum products. Most of the leading oil-producing countries have banded together in an association known as the Organization of Petroleum Exporting Countries (OPEC).

Sports

The United Kingdom sends competitors to many European and world sporting championships, as well as to the Commonwealth Games every four years. But the most high profile of all international sporting organizations is the International Olympic Committee (IOC). The IOC was

founded on 23 June 1894 by the French educator Baron Pierre de Coubertin. The IOC is an international non-governmental, non-profit body. Its primary responsibility is to supervise the organization of the summer and winter Olympic Games. The main purpose of the IOC and the Olympic Movement is to contribute to building a peaceful and better world by educating youth through sport, practised without discrimination of any kind and in the Olympic spirit, which requires mutual understanding, friendship, solidarity and fair play.

FIND OUT...

You can find out more about the International Olympic Committee at its website (www.olympic.org). It is not the only international sporting organization. FIFA is the world governing body for football (www.fifa.com). Almost every sport has its world association.

Olympic Games, like Sydney 2000, aim to promote friendship, as well as friendly rivalry, among the world community.

BUILDING A WORLD COMMUNITY
Getting the message across

The image of a country – especially as it is presented abroad – is an important factor in charting its future. One of the arguments in favour of retaining the British royal family is that state visits by the Queen or other family members raises Britain's influence and reputation.

But it requires more than simply sending the Queen abroad to paint a complete picture of modern life in Britain! A number of organizations, many of them funded by or linked to the Foreign and **Commonwealth** Office, provide the outside world with information about developments in the United Kingdom. The aim of such organizations is to provide goodwill, unprejudiced information and to improve cultural and educational relations.

Staying 'on message'

The World Service is a branch of the BBC that is aimed at foreign listeners. Unlike other elements of the BBC, which are funded through the income from TV licence fees, the World Service is **subsidized** by the FCO. This arrangement makes sense for two reasons. The first and rather obvious reason is that World Service broadcasts are not beamed into Britain, so it would be unfair to charge British listeners for a service that they cannot receive. Secondly, the World Service is playing an essential and well-respected role in furthering British interests abroad.

The World Service mission is to offer listeners a radio 'snapshot' of life in Britain, as well as to provide an internationally respected source of news. World Service broadcasts are a mix of BBC material from the other five stations as well as original broadcasts in dozens of foreign languages. By providing the only impartial source of news for people in war-torn countries, the World Service strengthens Britain's reputation as a first-class world power. The goodwill generated by these broadcasts is hard to measure, but many former rebel groups (such as the African National Congress in South Africa) express their gratitude to the World Service after they have succeeded in gaining power. This sense of warmth and solidarity in turn helps British firms in their trade relations with such countries.

British Council

The British Council terms itself as 'the United Kingdom's international organization for educational and cultural relations'. Its purpose is to enhance the UK's reputation as a valued partner in the world. The British Council creates an opportunity for people worldwide with programmes in education, English language teaching, the arts, science, governance and information, through a network of 243 offices and teaching centres in 110 countries.

The British Council receives a **grant-in-aid** from the FCO and earns additional income from teaching English, conducting British examinations and managing development and training contracts. By creating opportunities to connect with the latest skills, ideas and experience from the UK, the British Council aims to create lasting partnerships between Britain and other cultures.

Studying in Britain

The British Chevening Scholarships, funded by the FCO, are influential awards that enable overseas students to study in the United Kingdom. The scholarships are offered in more than 150 countries, and enable talented graduates and young professionals to become familiar with the UK and to gain skills that will benefit their countries. The Chevening programme currently provides around 2200 new scholarships each year, worth about £35 million, for postgraduate studies or research at UK institutions of higher education.

Rhodes Scholarships

Perhaps even more widely known throughout the world are the Rhodes Scholarships, which bring outstanding students from eighteen countries and five continents to the University of Oxford. The scholarships pay full tuition, living expenses and transport costs. Founded in 1902, and using the trust funds established by the statesman Cecil Rhodes, the Rhodes Scholarships are the oldest and most important honour a recent graduate can win. Because awards are made on the basis of versatility, leadership and social concern, as well as academic excellence, Rhodes scholars are counted among the most important people of their generation. The benefits to Britain are obvious, especially when you consider that Rhodes scholars (such as former US President Bill Clinton) can go on to hold influential decision-making positions in their own countries.

'Proven intellectual and academic achievement of a high standard is the first quality expected of applicants, but they will also be required to show integrity of character, interest in and respect for their fellow beings, the ability to lead and the energy to use their talents to the full.'

The BBC World Service reaches listeners in remote parts of the world, like this man in Burkina Faso, West Africa.

BUILDING A WORLD COMMUNITY
Look to the future

The United Kingdom is at a crossroads. In the next few decades, it will need to address how it presents itself to the modern world - the **global village** mentioned in the Introduction. This will be important because of the increased ties – economic, cultural and political – that shape the world today. The years since the end of the Second World War have given birth to the framework of organizations that link Britain to the rest of the world, but these organizations are changing, just as the United Kingdom itself is.

One of Britain's first concerns is to define itself. Is it to be a government of regions, taking the increased **self-determination** accorded to Scotland, Wales and Northern Ireland further? Already, some Scottish **nationalists** – who once argued for all-out independence – are proposing a reduction of the 'Britishness' of UK **sovereignty**, in favour of a European-wide continent of regions. Scotland of course would benefit, as would regions such as Catalonia, Bavaria and the Italian regions.

A young asylum seeker from Kosovo awaits processing at the UK Immigration Reception at Dover in Kent.

Whether or not the United Kingdom goes down that road, it must also reach a **consensus** about just what it means to be British. Decades of immigration from Britain's former colonies have produced a multi-cultural British society, particularly in the cities. But even in the early twenty-first century, there have been calls for a return to an 'undiluted', Anglo-Saxon, British culture. Britain must decide on how to reconcile such views – even if they are minority views – with maintaining credibility in truly multi-cultural bodies such as the United Nations. In a sense, Britain's contribution to – and benefits from – such international organizations will depend on the image it has of itself.

Lessons for others

Britain's hard-fought negotiations to promote peace in Northern Ireland have won praise from international observers. The UK has worked in exemplary fashion with its nearest neighbour – and long-time enemy – Ireland to fashion a system that recognizes differences while promoting consensus. The British should not ignore their ability to produce reasonable solutions in the face of those who seem unwilling to compromise. And it is the 'regional' conflicts, like that in Northern Ireland, that are likely to be the problem areas in the future. This experience will benefit other nations that seem torn by conflict.

A pear-shaped world?

There are many reasons to be pessimistic about the decades to come. Despite efforts in China, the world's most populated country, to curb its population growth, the number of people living on our planet could double by 2050 from its present figure of about 6 billion. Global warming and the damaged ozone layer in the atmosphere could change the climate forever, turning vast areas into desert and submerging many low-lying regions under water. The AIDS epidemic, already a terrible killer in Africa, shows no immediate signs of a cure. And despite the end of the Cold War, nuclear weapons still abound and are rumoured to be for sale on the **black market**. Coupled with the continuing threat of terrorism, the presence of these weapons is ominous.

These problems, and others we might not even know about, are on a global scale. The world will only arrive at their solutions through concerted effort. It is blinkered for any nationality to assume that the problems belong elsewhere in the world. The road ahead is indeed difficult, but thanks to the UK's continued involvement with global organizations, it can play an important role in addressing these concerns.

The decades since the last world war might have thrown up all of these new threats, but those same years saw the end to smallpox, polio and other diseases and the reduced likelihood of another conflict sweeping across the world. None of this progress could have come about without the hard work of international organizations. Contributing along the way was the work of British scientists and statesmen, athletes and accountants. And the United Kingdom, at the beginning of the twenty-first century, would be a poorer place without them.

DEBATE
Issues for discussion

Britain's role within the range of international organizations outlined in these pages depends on how well it copes with the lessons of the past in order to look to the future. Most of the historical events described in this book, as well as the descriptions of UK membership in global bodies, should provide you with ideas about what it means to be a citizen – both of the United Kingdom and of the wider world. A few of the more pressing questions are outlined below as starting points for such a discussion.

Does the Commonwealth still have a role to play in the modern world?

To many outside observers, the **Commonwealth** appears to be simply a remnant of the British Empire with no real purpose. Some would argue that maintaining strong links with the Commonwealth reduces the UK's role within other, more fully international, organizations. Do – and can – the Commonwealth's rulings carry any weight beyond the borders of the UK's foreign colonies? Does it matter if they do not, since the important thing is to establish common ground among very different nations?

Do close links with the United States affect UK relations with its European partners?

Many Prime Ministers since the Second World War have spoken of Britain's 'special relationship' with the United States. This issue is fundamental to the future of the United Kingdom and has consequences within British politics. The question assumes that closer links with one power (the United States) weaken links with the other (the EU), and vice versa. Need this be the case? And if the special relationship really exists, how does it benefit the UK, or is it simply a way for the United States to ensure that it has a compliant ally in an otherwise sceptical continent?

Does NATO still have a role in the world now that the Cold War is over?

NATO's history and organization is dominated by the fact that the UK and other Western nations feared a military build-up (and possible attack) by the Soviet Union and its allies. Through the years, many Europeans have felt that their continent would be the potential battlefield in such a conflict and that they – rather than the United States, which has always played a dominant role in NATO – should decide on how to preserve European security. With the Cold War over, and with it the need to rely on US arms and troops, many Europeans are arguing for a new EU-sponsored military force. Is this a rational next step in European security concerns, or would it bring new difficulties?

Should the government do more to help people in developing countries

Organizations such as Save the Children and Oxfam raise millions of pounds each year to help people in developing countries. But compared to many other European countries, the United Kingdom sends a relatively small proportion of aid to these countries. Should the government play a larger role in this process, or would that reduce the amount that charitable organizations might raise?

This question arose often during the period of Conservative government under Mrs Thatcher (1979–90). She believed in the rights (and duties) of individuals, and for her it was fitting that individuals shoulder the burden of sending aid abroad. Yet there has not been a sizeable increase in the government proportion of aid under Labour. Might they hold the same principles?

What lessons can be learned from the failure of the League of Nations to prevent the Second World War?

Limited by the US refusal to join and eventually ignored by many of its most powerful members, the League of Nations was powerless to stop the build-up of weapons in Germany and Italy, and the invasion of China by Japan. The Second World War was an inevitable consequence of these factors. Does the UN have enough power to prevent a repeat of such events?

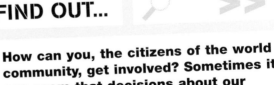

FIND OUT...

How can you, the citizens of the world community, get involved? Sometimes it can seem that decisions about our futures are made by huge organizations and we just have to live with them. But pressure groups that campaign for things they believe in can often make a difference. Greenpeace (www.greenpeace.org) and Friends of the Earth (www.foe.org.uk) aim to protect the environment, whilst Amnesty International (www.amnesty.org.uk) fights for human rights. Visit their websites and see how these groups are trying to change things for the world.

FURTHER RESOURCES

These pages provide you with a list of some of the most important international organizations of which the United Kingdom is a member. Most have websites. Not surprisingly, links from one site lead to others, so that the Web version of the organizations mirrors their interrelationships in real life.

Political

Foreign and Commonwealth Office

King Charles Street
London SW1A 2AH

www.fco.gov.uk

Government department set up to promote the national interests of the United Kingdom within the international arena. The website offers news, travel advice and information about the FCO, including details of UK overseas missions and the FCO families association.

The Commonwealth

www.thecommonwealth.org

This site offers an outline of the programs, projects, meetings and events, FAQ'S, publications, and journals, of the Commonwealth.

European Union (EU)

http://europa.eu.int/index.htm

General information about the EU, as well as official documents, publications, online services, statistics, directory of members and a searchable index.

United Nations

www.un.org

The main website (above) has many links to pages dealing with its peacekeeping operations. There are full listings of all UN missions along with maps, participating nations and mission briefings.

United Nations Children's Fund (UNICEF)

www.unicef.org

United Nations Educational, Scientific and Cultural Organization (UNESCO)

www.unesco.org

United Nations High Commission for Refugees (UNHCR)

www.unhcr.ch

Food and Agriculture Organization of the United Nations (FAO)

www.fao.org

Speeches, seminars, workshops, publications and programmes, press releases, databases, search engine, publications, statistics, conferences, directories and other related information.

World Health Organization (WHO)

www.who.int

Economics and trade

International Labour Organization (ILO)

www.ilo.org

The ILO site discusses international labour standards and human rights, in addition to offering ILO press reports, speeches, programme topics, a listing of department home pages and a great deal of other information.

International Monetary Fund (IMF)

www.imf.org

On the IMF site you can find general information on the IMF as well as links to the IMF institute and the Joint World Bank-IMF Library.

World Trade Organization

www.wto.org

The site gives a full account of the history and workings of the WTA, as established by the World Trade Organization/General Agreement on Tariffs and Trade in 1994.

Military

North Atlantic Treaty Organization (NATO)

www.nato.int

The official NATO homepage features press releases, fact sheets, publications and historic documents, on-line library, speeches, reports and related sites.

Organization for Security and Cooperation in Europe (OSCE)

www.osce.org

This site offers general information about the organization, a list of participating states, budgeting information, newsletter, press releases, permanent council journals and decisions, information on the mission to Bosnia and Herzegovina and upcoming events.

Justice

The International Court of Justice

www.icj-cij.org

This website provides information on the procedures, jurisdiction, enforcement and other important features of the ICJ.

Miscellaneous

Amnesty International

www.amnesty.org

Amnesty International is a human rights organization that supports the Universal Declaration of Human Rights created in 1948 after the Second World War. The website provides information on the organization and how to get involved.

International Committee of the Red Cross and Red Crescent (ICRC)

www.icrc.org

The Red Cross, which operates under the name the Red Crescent in Muslim countries, provides much-needed medical and development assistance in 176 countries where people have suffered from natural disasters as well as destructive conflicts.

International Olympic Committee
Château de Vidy
Case Postale 356
1007 Lausanne
Switzerland

www.olympic.org

Organization that governs the Olympics, including choosing where they are held and what sports are included.

Oxfam

Oxfam House
274 Banbury Road
Oxford OX2 7DZ

www.oxfam.org

A development, relief and campaigning organization working to find lasting solutions to world poverty. The website has details on how to get involved in Oxfam campaigns.

The British Council

10, Spring Gardens
London SW1A 2BN
Telephone 020 7930 8466
Fax 020 7389 6347

www.britishcouncil.org

The British Council promotes educational and cultural exchange with other countries. The website has information on the council's projects in the arts, sciences, education and how to get involved here or in the projects abroad which include teaching English or helping to improve governance abroad.

Further reading

A Global Agenda: Issues before the 53rd General Assembly of the United Nations, edited by John Tessitore and Susan Woolfson. Lanham: Rowman and Littlefield, 1998.

International Politics, fourth edition, edited by Robert J. Art and Robert Jervis. New York: Harper Collins, 1996.

Organizations that help the world: United Nations, by Michael Pollard. Watford, UK: Exley Publications, 1993

Politics and Policy in the European Union, third edition, by Stephen George. Oxford: Oxford University Press, 1996.

The United Nations: International Organization and World Politics, second edition, by Robert E. Riggs and Jack C. Plano. Fort Worth: Harcourt Brace, 1994.

INDEX

Titles in the *Citizen's Guide* series include:

Hardback   0 431 14493 1

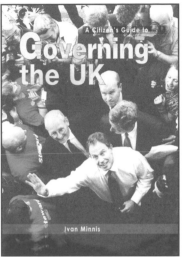

Hardback   0 431 14492 3

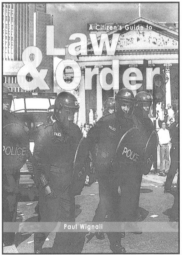

Hardback   0 431 14495 8

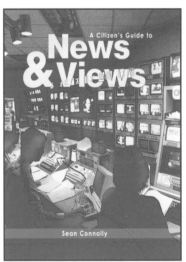

Hardback   0 431 14491 5

Hardback   0 431 14494 X

Hardback   0 431 14490 7

Find out about the other titles in this series on our website www.heinemann.co.uk/library